The Caterpillar Story

Alex Ramsay and Paul Humphrey

Illustrated by

Katy Sleight

Evans

5

They are young caterpillars.

7

Yes, but you must look after it properly.

I'll bring in some of the leaves you found it on.

11

My caterpillar has lots of legs.

They help it to cling on to the plants it eats.

As it grows, a caterpillar changes its skin.

He's eaten a lot of leaves.

17

18

He has
started to
change. Just
wait and see.

19

20

It has turned into a chrysalis.
What happens next is very
exciting.

22

And look what's coming out.

23

Yes, and now it's drying its wings in the sunshine.

It's ready to fly away now.
Open the window.

27

It's going out to find some flowers. Soon it will lay eggs and what will come out of the eggs?

28

More caterpillars!

Here are the stages in the caterpillar story. How many of them can you remember?